DON'T LAUGH CHALLENGE®

Joke Book

STOCKING STUFFER
EDITION

VOL. 3

An Interactive Holiday Game Book for Boys and Girls Ages 6-12 Years Old

TM & Copyright© 2020 by Bacchus Publishing House™
ALL RIGHTS RESERVED.
Published in the United States. By purchase of this book, you have been licensed one copy for personal use only. No part of this work may be reproduced, redistributed, or used in any form or by any means without prior written permission of the publisher and copyright owner.
The Don't Laugh Challenge®

TX 8-837-630
TX 8-837-124
www.dontlaughchallenge.com

Don't Laugh Challenge
BONUS PLAY

Join our Joke Club and get the Bonus Play PDF!

Simply send us an email to:

bacchuspublish@gmail.com

and you will get the following:

- 10 BONUS hilarious jokes!
- An entry in our Monthly Giveaway of a $25 Amazon Gift card!

We draw a new winner each month and will contact you via email!
Good luck!

Welcome to The Don't Laugh Challenge® Stocking Stuffer Edition Vol. 3

🍭 How do you play?

The Don't Laugh Challenge is made up of 10 rounds with 2 games in each round. It is a 2-3 player game with the players being Player 1 and Player 2, with an optional King or Queen. In each game you have an opportunity to score points by making the other players laugh!

After completing each round, tally up the points to determine the Round Champion! After completing all 10 rounds, add up all your round totals together to see who will be crowned the **ULTIMATE DON'T LAUGH CHALLENGE MASTER!** If you end up in a tie, use our final Tie-Breaker Round for a Winner Takes All!

🍭 Who can play the game?

Get the whole family involved! Grab a family member or a friend and take turns going back and forth. We've also added Bonus Points in game 2, so grab a 3rd person (a.k.a. King or Queen) and earn an extra point by making them guess your scene!

✦ **Tip** ✦

Make any of the activities extra funny by using facial expressions, funny voices or silly movements!

Welcome to The Don't Laugh Challenge® Stocking Stuffer Edition Vol. 3

🎄 **Game 1 - Jokes (1 point each)**
Player 1 will hold the book and read each joke to Player 2. If the joke or the player's delivery makes Player 2 laugh, Player 1 records a point for the joke. After the jokes, follow the guided instructions at the bottom of the page to continue on to Game 2!

🎄 **Game 2 - Silly Scenarios (2 points each + BONUS point)**
Without telling the other Player what the scenarios say, read each scenario to yourself and then get creative by acting it out! You can use sound effects, but be sure not to say any words! If you make the other Player laugh, record your points and continue to the next scenario!

✦ **BONUS POINT** ✦
Get the King or Queen to guess the scene and/or what you're acting out correctly, and you score a BONUS POINT!

LET'S GET STARTED! ➔

Jokes

PLAYER 1

What do elderly elves use to walk better?

Candy canes!

___ /1

How did Rudolph feel when he found out his nose could glow?

En-LIGHT-ened.

___ /1

What's a good, quick meal in the North Pole?

Santa's Hamburger Helper.

___ /1

How do you start a virtual fire in an online chimney?

You have to enter the LOG-in!

___ /1

JOKES TOTAL: ___ /4

PLAYER 1 CONTINUE TO THE NEXT PAGE ➡

Silly Scenarios

(Act it out!)

PLAYER 1

You're Santa Claus, but unfortunately you got a cold. You try getting out three strong, "*Ho, Ho, Ho's*", but you can't seem to get through them all without violently coughing. Try 2-3 times then blow your nose and give up!

/2

You're stirring a pot of delicious gravy for Christmas dinner and boy, does it smell **GOOD!** Right after you finish stirring, your hunger takes over! Grab the pot of gravy and pour the the whole thing on your head, then lick your lips and end with a big smile on your face! YUM!

/2

SILLY SCENARIOS TOTAL: ___ /4

NOW, PASS THE BOOK TO PLAYER 2 ➔

Jokes

PLAYER 2

What's the difference between reindeer and kids on Christmas?

For kids, the toughest part is the WAIT.
For reindeer, it's the WEIGHT!   /1

Where does Santa keep a spare key to his workshop?

Under a *Jingle Bell Rock!*   /1

Which Christmas play focuses on mini-golf?

The PUTT-cracker.   /1

What is Santa's favorite kind of cereal?

Cookie Crisp.   /1

JOKES TOTAL: /4

PLAYER 2 CONTINUE TO THE NEXT PAGE ➡

Silly Scenarios

(Act it out!)

PLAYER 2

Take off your left sock. Sniff it, then sneeze! Put your right hand in it, then pull out your hand and voila! A COOKIE! Eat the cookie and then put your sock back on like nothing happened.

/2

You're an elf who's taking some time off and focusing on getting in shape! You're doing stand-up sit-ups, but very slowly. Each time you come up, you let out a little elf-like grunt. Then, you're grunts turn into "*I...need... a candy cane*" until you *pretend* collapse on the floor! Looks like you just love candy too much!

/2

SILLY SCENARIOS TOTAL: _____ /4

TIME TO SCORE YOUR POINTS ➡

PLAYER 1   /8
ROUND TOTAL

PLAYER 2   /8
ROUND TOTAL

Round Winner

Jokes

PLAYER 1

What kind of hammer likes sliding on the snow?
SLED-ge hammer. /1

Which Halloween creature decorates for Christmas?
The Grim WREATH-er! /1

How did the boy know he was getting a cat as a present?
He had a good FELINE! /1

What kind of Christmas trees do you put in a museum?
ART-ificial ones. /1

JOKES TOTAL: /4

PLAYER 1 CONTINUE TO THE NEXT PAGE →

Silly Scenarios

(Act it out!)

PLAYER 1

You're sledding down a snowy hill! Sit down on the floor, and yell "*WOOSH!*" as you raise your arms and sniff your armpits! Once you get a whiff - Woah, are they STINKY! Fall off your sled from the stench and start rolling down the hill!

/2

Stomp your feet to the beat of *Jingle Bell Rock!* Shake your hips every fourth stop, nod your head every sixth stop, and clap your hands every second stomp! (Don't worry, it takes practice!)

/2

SILLY SCENARIOS TOTAL: ___ /4

NOW, PASS THE BOOK TO PLAYER 2 ➡

Jokes

PLAYER 2

What happens when a fairy toilet is broken?
They call the sugarplum-ber!

/1

Where do cars hang their stockings for Santa?
Over the TIRE-place.

/1

Why don't basketball referees like the holidays?
Too much TRAVELING.

/1

What happened when the Little Drummer Boy forgot his drums?
He just *"per hum, hum, hum, hummed!"*

/1

JOKES TOTAL: ___ /4

PLAYER 2 CONTINUE TO THE NEXT PAGE →

Silly Scenarios

(Act it out!)

PLAYER 2

You're decorating the Christmas tree, but as soon as you put anything on the tree the decorations just fall right down! Continue picking them up and putting them back on the tree a few times, then you get so annoyed that you EXPLODE with frustration!

_____/2

You're a reindeer (use your hands and fingers on your head to signify your antlers) and you've decided to join the Christmas carolers. However, you're a reindeer so your singing to *Jingle Bells* sounds more like moaning and groaning! Show them how it's done!

_____/2

SILLY SCENARIOS TOTAL: _____ /4

TIME TO SCORE YOUR POINTS ➡

PLAYER 1

/8

_____
ROUND TOTAL

PLAYER 2

/8

_____
ROUND TOTAL

_____
Round Winner

Jokes

PLAYER 1

Why is it best to wear winter clothing while eating a big meal?
It makes it easier to SCARF down!   /1

What do horses put in front of their churches on Christmas?
NEIGH-tivity Scenes.   /1

Why don't elves go to school?
Every day is a snow day!   /1

What do you call Christmas cookies that have only been partially eaten?
INJURE-bread men!   /1

JOKES TOTAL: /4

PLAYER 1 CONTINUE TO THE NEXT PAGE ➡

Silly Scenarios

(Act it out!)

PLAYER 1

You're in the middle of a *slow motion* snowball fight! Throw the snowballs, dodge snowballs, and get hit with snowballs - ALL in slow motion! Don't forget to make funny faces as you get hit, too!

_____/2

You just finished baking Christmas cookies for Santa! Open the oven and grab the cookies- "*YOWCH!*" They are HOT! Juggle the cookies while you use random sound effects to show how hot they are!

_____/2

SILLY SCENARIOS TOTAL: _____ /4

NOW, PASS THE BOOK TO PLAYER 2 ➡

Jokes

PLAYER 2

What did the police yell at Frosty when he was running away?

"Freeze!"

___/1

If the stork delivers babies on every other day, who delivers them on Christmas?

The Candy Crane.

___/1

What's a cat's favorite part of the Christmas tree?

The string lights!

___/1

Which tool likes Christmas the least?

The SCREW-ge Driver.

___/1

JOKES TOTAL: ___/4

PLAYER 2 CONTINUE TO THE NEXT PAGE ➔

Silly Scenarios

(Act it out!)

PLAYER 2

Time for some fun DIY Christmas decorations! Use your hands and fingers as a pair of scissors and stick your tongue out to concentrate as you make as many *pretend* decorations as possible within 15 seconds! Ready... GO!

/2

You are in a snowball fight AGAINST YOURSELF! Make snowballs! Get hit by snowballs! Dodge snowballs! EAT A SNOWBALL! Mumble, "Merry Christmas!"

/2

SILLY SCENARIOS TOTAL: _____ /4

TiME TO SCORE YOUR POINTS ➡

PLAYER 1

/8

_____

ROUND TOTAL

PLAYER 2

/8

_____

ROUND TOTAL

Round Winner
_____

Jokes

PLAYER 1

Why did the Christmas ham stay up so late to see Santa?
He was determined to MEAT him!

___/1

What's an elf's favorite cereal?
Frosted Snowflakes.

___/1

If the Polar Express comes in the winter, what comes in the summer?
The Solar Express!

___/1

What does Santa say when his sleigh goes in reverse?
"Oh, Oh, Oh!"

___/1

JOKES TOTAL: ___/4

PLAYER 1 CONTINUE TO THE NEXT PAGE ➡

Silly Scenarios
(Act it out!)

PLAYER 1

You are going to play a Christmas carol on the piano, but you have absolutely no clue on how to play. Play frantically, as your fingers dance all over the place! Act confident and hopefully, no one questions you...

___/2

Lie down on the floor and make snoring sounds to show you're asleep. You wake up because you're so excited about Christmas morning, and can't fall asleep again! Roll around from side to side... What's that sound?! Santa?! Nope. Flop back down and go back to sleep.

___/2

SILLY SCENARIOS TOTAL: ___/4

NOW, PASS THE BOOK TO PLAYER 2 ➡

Jokes

PLAYER 2

What has a shell and flies?
Turtle dove.

/1

How much of addition is in the answer?
SUM of it!

/1

What did Santa Claus say when he met a pirate?
"Yo, Ho, Ho, Ho!"

/1

Who is the sweetest person that lives at the North Pole?

/1

The Gingerbread man!

JOKES TOTAL: ___ /4

PLAYER 2 CONTINUE TO THE NEXT PAGE →

Silly Scenarios

(Act it out!)   **PLAYER 2**

You're opening a present, and you're so excited about it because you already know what it is. It's a wooden stick horse! After getting off the wrapping paper, you put the horse between your legs and gallop around the room with one hand in the air. YEEHAW!!!

/2

Mmm, nothing like hot cocoa on a cold day! As you take a sip, you nearly jump out of your seat! That is HOT!!! Fan your mouth and wait a few seconds, then do it again and make this reaction even more dramatic!

/2

SILLY SCENARIOS TOTAL: _____ /4

TIME TO SCORE YOUR POINTS ➡

PLAYER 1   /8
                ———————
                ROUND TOTAL

PLAYER 2   /8
                ———————
                ROUND TOTAL

———————————
Round Winner

Jokes

PLAYER 1

What do you call a reindeer who makes Santa snacks?
Cookie DOE! /1

Who knows everything and is always nice?
Alexa. /1

Why didn't the shoeless Eskimo want to fight the polar bear?
He got cold feet! /1

What do sheep say to each other during the holiday season?
"Merry Christmas to EWE!" /1

JOKES TOTAL: ___ /4

PLAYER 1 CONTINUE TO THE NEXT PAGE →

Silly Scenarios

(Act it out!)

PLAYER 1

You're auditioning to become the next mall Santa, but you can't seem to get the iconic laugh right! Using your best deep voice, say the following: *"Hooh! Haah! Heeh! HEY! Hooba hooba! HEEEW! Holla! HOW HOW HOW!"* Until FINALLY, you master the classic "Ho! Ho! Ho!"

/2

Knock, Knock! Knock on your neighbors door and get ready to sing some Christmas carols! Clear your throat, but as soon as you're about to sing there's only one problem... you're mute! Mime your favorite Christmas tune instead to give your neighbors the most unique Christmas carol ever!

/2

SILLY SCENARIOS TOTAL: ____ /4

NOW, PASS THE BOOK TO PLAYER 2 ➡

Jokes

PLAYER 2

Why didn't the elves believe Santa could make it down the chimney?
They thought he was blowing smoke!   /1

What sounds like *wood*, but is only around when you're not naughty?
Good!   /1

Where do you find a hammer, a chisel, and 100 elves?
Santa's workshop!   /1

What kind of horse is always grateful to receive presents on Christmas?
A gift horse.   /1

JOKES TOTAL: ___ /4

PLAYER 2 CONTINUE TO THE NEXT PAGE ➔

Silly Scenarios

(Act it out!)

PLAYER 2

Mistletoe ALERT! As you walk under a mistletoe, pretend to make our with yourself under it! Face your back towards everyone with your arms crossed and moving up and down behind your back (to make it look like someone is with you). Do this for a few seconds then stop and point above you to let everyone know there's a mistletoe and you take the rule VERY seriously!

_____ /2

There's frost on the light pole in front of you. You decide to give it a lick, but now your tongue is STUCK! Flail your arms and try to yell "*HELP!*" but it just comes out as mumbled gibberish since your tongue is still sticking out!

_____ /2

SILLY SCENARIOS TOTAL: _____ /4

TIME TO SCORE YOUR POINTS ➡

PLAYER 1

/8

_____

ROUND TOTAL

PLAYER 2

/8

_____

ROUND TOTAL

_____

Round Winner

Jokes

PLAYER 1

What's another name for a stocking stuffer?
A foot.

___/1

How does Santa make it over the ocean?
He uses the yule-TIDES!

___/1

What's the rainforest's favorite Christmas song?
JUNGLE Bells.

___/1

What did the snowman say when he heard a clever joke?
"Ah, ICY what you did there!"

___/1

JOKES TOTAL: ___/4

PLAYER 1 CONTINUE TO THE NEXT PAGE ➡

Silly Scenarios

(Act it out!)

PLAYER 1

You're playing hockey on a frozen lake, and you've got the puck! You're making moves - spinning around defenders, skating forward and showing everyone up! As the goal is coming near you smack a slap shot and... GOAL! Cheer for your team and throw in a little victory dance!

/2

You're in the middle of a snowball fight! Make a HUGE snowball, but it's so heavy that you have to use both arms to carry it around! Now lift it up and drop it on one of your pretend friends and laugh!

/2

SILLY SCENARIOS TOTAL: ___ /4

NOW, PASS THE BOOK TO PLAYER 2 ➡

Jokes

PLAYER 2

Why do pirates love Christmas?
X-mas the spot!

/1

What do you buy, then cover, then give away?
Presents.

/1

What did the reindeer say when Santa told a joke?
"You sleigh me!"

/1

How does the Grim Reaper decorate for Christmas?
With Ice-SICKLES!

/1

JOKES TOTAL: /4

PLAYER 2 CONTINUE TO THE NEXT PAGE →

Silly Scenarios

(Act it out!)

PLAYER 2

You got the brilliant idea of giving yourself as the present this year! Wrap yourself in gift wrapping paper from head to toe, then tie a big ribbon on the top of your head! Perfect. Now, stay very still and as soon as your *pretend* family walks in, jump up to rip your body from the paper and yell "*SURPRISE!*"

/2

It's Christmas morning, so that means it's time to open your Christmas present! The excitement is just too much to handle! GASP, clap your hands together, stand up, then clap your thighs twice! Jump on one leg! Twirl around! And for the grand finale... Imitate a dolphin sound!

/2

SILLY SCENARIOS TOTAL: _____ /4

TIME TO SCORE YOUR POINTS ➔

PLAYER 1

/8

ROUND TOTAL

PLAYER 2

/8

ROUND TOTAL

Round Winner

Jokes

PLAYER 1

What Christmas treat do they eat on islands?
Sandy canes!

___/1

How do eggs benedict greet each other during Christmas?
"Happy Hollandaise!"

___/1

What do you call gloves that are happy you picked them?
Smittens!

___/1

Why do houses that are painted well thrive in the cold?
They're well COAT-ed!

___/1

JOKES TOTAL: ___/4

PLAYER 1 CONTINUE TO THE NEXT PAGE ➡

Silly Scenarios

(Act it out!)

PLAYER 1

You're doing some last-minute Christmas shopping! Push the trolley around with a confident look on your face! Put as many things in the trolley as possible, and look surprised every time you spot a new item! Now that the trolley is full, it's... so... HEAVY!!!

/2

You're quite a busy elf! Wrap presents as fast as you can - Grab the boxes, wrap them quickly, then tie a bow and repeat! You're going so fast that you didn't even notice your hair is on FIRE! Do your best not to slow down, and try to put out the fire between wrapping presents!

/2

SILLY SCENARIOS TOTAL: _____ /4

NOW, PASS THE BOOK TO PLAYER 2 ➡

Jokes

PLAYER 2

What do fish hang on their doors for Christmas?
Reefs! /1

What do Eskimos use to make crafts?
Igloo sticks. /1

On which day in December can you listen to a dozen drummers?
The 12th Day of Christmas. /1

What are pastries called in the North Pole?
/1

Santa claws!

JOKES TOTAL: /4

PLAYER 2 CONTINUE TO THE NEXT PAGE ➡

Silly Scenarios

(Act it out!)

PLAYER 2

You're eating a delicious Christmas dinner. Make smacking and slurping noises while eating, until you accidentally get something stuck in your teeth! Make a weird face and use one finger to really get in there and get it out... Ah, got it! Examine it, then toss it and keep eating!

_____ /2

You are so excited about Christmas that you spontaneously start to hum *Jingle Bells* while hopping with one foot and your arms raised above your head!

_____ /2

SILLY SCENARIOS TOTAL: _____ /4

TIME TO SCORE YOUR POINTS ➡

PLAYER 1

/8

ROUND TOTAL

PLAYER 2

/8

ROUND TOTAL

Round Winner

Jokes

PLAYER 1

What winter sport is for those who don't like Christmas?
The *Scrooge* Luge.

/1

How do you know that Christmas stars are jealous of Christmas trees?
They're always trying to TOP them!

/1

What dirt dweller doesn't like Christmas?
The Gr-INCH worm.

/1

If Santa lived underwater, who would lead his sleigh?
Ru-DOLPHIN!

/1

JOKES TOTAL: ___ /4

PLAYER 1 CONTINUE TO THE NEXT PAGE ➡

Silly Scenarios

(Act it out!)

PLAYER 1

You're a lumberjack and your job is to cut down the perfect Christmas tree! Hum to the tune of We Wish You a Merry Christmas while chopping away on the defenseless little tree... with your FEET!

/2

You decide to break a very weird world record, the record of how many Christmas presents you can balance on your head at once! Pick a present from the floor and put it on your head, and continue with a few presents! Make sure you keep your tongue sticking out of the side of your mouth the entire time to enhance concentration!

/2

SILLY SCENARIOS TOTAL: ___ /4

NOW, PASS THE BOOK TO PLAYER 2 ➡

Jokes

PLAYER 2

Why are thrift stores open to everyone during the Christmas season?
It is GOODWILL to all! /1

What happened after the elf snuck into the gift loading area?
He was sacked! /1

Why did Mrs. Claus buy so much pre-made cookie dough?
Because it was KNEAD-ed! /1

What spice did the chef get on the first day of Christmas? /1
A Parsnip in a Pantry!

JOKES TOTAL: ___/4

PLAYER 2 CONTINUE TO THE NEXT PAGE →

Silly Scenarios

(Act it out!)

PLAYER 2

It's snowing, and you're making snow angels on the ground. For some reason, you were taught to make them face down, so your face in the snow while you do it. You come up with a big smile and mouthful of snow, then you spit it out! Get up and admire your good looking snow angel!

/2

Describe your favorite Christmas memory by only using sound effects and interpretive dance! Ready... GO!

/2

SILLY SCENARIOS TOTAL: _____ /4

TIME TO SCORE YOUR POINTS ➔

PLAYER 1   /8

                 ROUND TOTAL

PLAYER 2   /8

                 ROUND TOTAL

Round Winner

Jokes

PLAYER 1

Why was the surprise gift for Mrs. Claus ruined?
The cat was out of the bag!

___/1

What do gifts say when their name is called for attendance?
"*Present!*"

___/1

Why couldn't the quiet elf say what he wanted?
He wasn't ALOUD.

___/1

What did Santa get the archer for Christmas?
Arrows with a BOW on top!

___/1

JOKES TOTAL: ___/4

PLAYER 1 CONTINUE TO THE NEXT PAGE ➡

Silly Scenarios

(Act it out!)

PLAYER 1

You're a nutcracker, and you are assigned to crack all the nuts for the dinner preparations. You grab a nut, put it into your mouth, and reach behind you to pull on your lever (which opens and closes your mouth), crunching each nut! Continue to crack the nuts, until UH-OH! Your lever got stuck so your mouth is stuck wide open!

/2

You're Rudolph the red-nosed reindeer! Get on all fours to walk around as you wait for Santa to finish up so you can deliver toys. While you're waiting, playfully tease and mess with the other reindeer by pulling their tail or tapping them on the shoulder then looking the other way! Afterall, you're just trying to have fun!

/2

SILLY SCENARIOS TOTAL: ____ /4

NOW, PASS THE BOOK TO PLAYER 2 ➡

Jokes

PLAYER 2

What is Santa's favorite kind of fish?

STAR-fish.

/1

What do you tell someone who is going to multiple Christmas parties?

"Have a VARY Merry Christmas!"

/1

Who stayed up late in the castles to see if they could spot Santa?

Silent knights!

/1

What do snowmen eat for breakfast?

Frosted Flakes.

/1

JOKES TOTAL: ___ /4

PLAYER 2 CONTINUE TO THE NEXT PAGE ➔

Silly Scenarios

(Act it out!) **PLAYER 2**

You're Santa, and you just got a brand new bag! You're carrying the bag over your shoulder like a model, looking over at it constantly with raised eyebrows letting out "*ooh's*" and "*aah's.*" You take the bag off your shoulder and flop it onto the ground where you brush your hand past it a few times like you're dusting it off, and really trying to emphasize the bag's flair like a fashion model! One more spin, then catwalk away with the bag behind your back!

/2

You're the Christmas tree. Stand straight and make a triangular shape with your body! However, the Christmas carols are so groovy you just have to dance **WITH YOUR LEGS MADE OUT OF JELLY!**

/2

SILLY SCENARIOS TOTAL: /4

TiME TO SCORE YOUR POiNTS ➔

PLAYER 1   /8
ROUND TOTAL

PLAYER 2   /8
ROUND TOTAL

Round Winner

Jokes

PLAYER 1

What do you call candy canes that are hung on the Christmas tree?
Orna-MINTS.

___ /1

In *Oz*, what does the Tin Man use to decorate the tree?
TIN-sel!

___ /1

How do snowflakes exercise?
They ride b-ICICLES!

___ /1

What's a great Valentine's gift in the North Pole?
Hot chocolate!

___ /1

JOKES TOTAL: ___ /4

PLAYER 1 CONTINUE TO THE NEXT PAGE ➡

Silly Scenarios

(Act it out!)  **PLAYER 1**

You're shoveling snow off of the driveway with a big shovel. You scrape it and throw it off to the side, scrape it and throw it off to the side again. But then you step on a patch of ice and slip, *dramatically* flying onto your back! OUCH!!!

_____/2

You're an elf, but you don't speak English. Instead, you speak high-pitched elf murmur. You're on the toy line making toys, and you're grumpy about being overworked, so you complain to the other elves and use your language with some elf attitude!

_____/2

SILLY SCENARIOS TOTAL: _____/4

NOW, PASS THE BOOK TO PLAYER 2 ➡

Jokes

PLAYER 2

What do baseball players get their ducks for Christmas?
Foul balls!

/1

What cycle cannot be ridden?
An icicle.

/1

Why does Poseidon's kid like Christmas time?
They are both the happiest SEA-son!

/1

What did the delivery man do when he delivered his packages?
Five frozen rings.

/1

JOKES TOTAL: /4

PLAYER 2 CONTINUE TO THE NEXT PAGE ➜

Silly Scenarios

(Act it out!)   PLAYER 2

You're baking cookies in the oven. You bend down to open the oven and give the smell that comes out a nice, big whiff. You're so excited that you grab the burning hot cookie pan with your bare hands! Oh no! You drop the cookies and pan! Hold your hand up in the air and in front of your face to show the painful agony!

_____ /2

Your index finger has been transformed into a candy cane by an elf! Go, "*WOAH!*" and make a hook shape with your finger and start licking it!

_____ /2

SILLY SCENARIOS TOTAL: _____ /4

TIME TO SCORE YOUR POINTS ➔

PLAYER 1

/8

___

ROUND TOTAL

PLAYER 2

/8

___

ROUND TOTAL

___

Round Winner

ADD UP ALL YOUR POINTS FROM EACH ROUND. THE PLAYER WITH THE MOST POINTS IS CROWNED THE ULTIMATE DON'T LAUGH CHALLENGE MASTER!

IN THE EVENT OF A TIE, CONTINUE TO THE ROUND 11 FOR THE TIE-BREAKER ROUND!

PLAYER 1 — GRAND TOTAL

PLAYER 2 — GRAND TOTAL

THE ULTIMATE DON'T LAUGH CHALLENGE MASTER

Jokes

PLAYER 1

Where does Thor send his letters to Santa?
The Norse Pole.

_____ /1

What's an elf's favorite fruit?
Sugarplum!

_____ /1

Why do jingle bells always have their holiday photoshoots during the winter?
They look dashing through the snow!

_____ /1

What's the main ingredient in Santa's salads?
ICEBERG lettuce.

_____ /1

JOKES TOTAL: _____ /4

PLAYER 1 CONTINUE TO THE NEXT PAGE →

Silly Scenarios

(Act it out!)

PLAYER 1

You're Santa Claus! You have just entered a family's home through the chimney and have to be super quiet! Sneak around like a ninja by rolling on the floor, dropping off some presents then tip-toeing your way to the milk and cookies! Eat the cookies, drink the milk, and smack your belly from happiness! Time to get out of here!

/2

You and a family member are battling over the last present with no name on. This means it's time for TUG-OF-WAR!!! Grunt and wheeze viciously as you try to get that present from them! After some battling, plop down to the ground and look down... looks like you won this time!

/2

SILLY SCENARIOS TOTAL: ___ /4

NOW, PASS THE BOOK TO PLAYER 2 ➡

Jokes

PLAYER 2

What is a dog's favorite candy?
Lolli-PUPS.

/1

Why couldn't the snowman get home for dinner?
He was snowed under at work!

/1

What is purple, has big teeth, five eyes and huge claws?
I don't know, but I hope it isn't hiding under my bed!

/1

What did the one-eyed pirate say when Santa asked if he'd like to have a gift?
"*Wood eye!*" (Would I!)

/1

JOKES TOTAL: /4

PLAYER 2 CONTINUE TO THE NEXT PAGE ➡

Silly Scenarios

(Act it out!)   **PLAYER 2**

You're warming your hands up by the fire, rubbing them together and making them nice and toasty. You get your feet in there, too. Ah, that feels nice! You close your eyes and relax, but then something starts to smell funny, like something is burning. You open your eyes and notice that **YOUR FEET ARE ON FIRE!!!** You spastically pat them out with your hands and blow to get those flames off!

_____/2

Time for some sledding fun! Sit down on the ground to show you're on your sled, then raise your arms and yell "*Woohoo!*" as you make your way down the hill! Uh-oh, you're going faster and faster... QUICK! Throw your body off to the side so you can finally stop!

_____/2

SILLY SCENARIOS TOTAL: _____/4

TIME TO SCORE YOUR POINTS ➔

ADD UP ALL YOUR POINTS FROM THE PREVIOUS ROUND. THE PLAYER WITH THE MOST POINTS IS CROWNED
THE ULTIMATE DON'T LAUGH CHALLENGE MASTER!

PLAYER 1 /8 ROUND TOTAL

PLAYER 2 /8 ROUND TOTAL

_____

THE ULTIMATE DON'T LAUGH CHALLENGE MASTER

CHECK OUT OUR

VISIT US AT
WWW.DONTLAUGHCHALLENGE.COM
TO CHECK OUT OUR NEWEST BOOKS!

OTHER JOKE BOOKS!

IF YOU HAVE ENJOYED OUR BOOK, WE WOULD LOVE FOR YOU TO REVIEW US ON AMAZON!

Made in the USA
Coppell, TX
10 December 2020